Bríd Cummins

1956–2004

Bríd Cummins

meters

Foreword: Catherine Connolly
Afterword: Rita Ann Higgins

ARLEN
HOUSE

The moral rights of the author have been asserted

First published in 2006 by
Arlen House
PO Box 222
Galway
Ireland
Phone/fax 086 8207617
arlenhouse@gmail.com

ISBN 1–903631–89–0, paperback

€10.00

Typesetting: Arlen House
Printed by: Betaprint, Dublin

162,503

ACKNOWLEDGEMENTS

Angela Harte and the Cummins family
Councillor Catherine Connolly, former Mayor of Galway
Rita Ann Higgins
The Arts Council / An Chomhairle Ealaíon

CONTENTS

Councillor Catherine Connolly

I consider it an honour and a very special privilege to write an introduction to this extraordinary book of poetry. Bríd's death, the lead up to it, and the circumstances surrounding it, have left an indelible mark on all of us, and on Galway as a city. That the book is being published one year to the day when we learned that Bríd was no longer with us is particularly poignant.

Aptly, of course, the book allows us to remember Bríd, to celebrate her life and creativity, but also to acknowledge her courage and persistence, despite the pain which was an integral part of her life. Most significantly, however, the publication of her poetry provides some redress to the appalling one-dimensional portrayal of Bríd by some elements of the media, and by some people in positions of power and influence, both prior to and subsequent to her death.

Unbelievably one year after the sad and tragic death of Bríd, there has been no enquiry — public or otherwise. What we have are two reports from Galway City Council, together with answers to 210 questions specifically submitted by a small number of City Councillors. One would have expected, or at least certainly hoped, that the two reports and 210 answers would have, in some way, enlightened us as to how decisions were made, including decisions:

not to grant Bríd a transfer.

to issue proceedings to evict her.

to issue proceedings to bar her.

to issue instructions to the emergency services not to house her.

to send what can only be described as bizarre e-mails prior to and on the day she was found dead.

to allow a City Council Meeting to proceed at 7pm on the very night she had already been discovered dead in her home unbeknownst to the then Mayor and City Councillors.

to mention only some of the more pertinent and detrimental decisions made.

Rather than enlightenment, however, the language and content of the reports and answers supplied have, in my opinion, served only to obfuscate, to evade, to ignore, to justify, to defer, and most tellingly of all, to exonerate. Moreover, the absence of senior management officials from Galway City Council and the absence of any representative from any of the homeless organisations in the city at the recent inquest into Bríd's death was in reality a potent absence.

What type of society have we become when a person's life and death can be treated in such a manner? What are the consequences for the person directly concerned, and for society generally, of the repeated and restrictive use of language and labels to describe that person's behaviour and/or a given problem? What is the value we now place on human life and human discourse? These questions, amongst others, are ones which must be addressed by all of us, given that actions are taken and language is used in our name.

It seems to me that this special book has already gently compelled us into that inevitable process of questioning, exploring and articulating alternative options and visions of what was, is and might be possible. Through her poems, Bríd's voice speaks to us directly and shares with us the wonderful complexity that is humanity. In hearing her voice the challenge now, of course, is to hear our own voices and to use them to reclaim our city.

Embracing that challenge would be a most fitting tribute to Bríd, a very special and talented woman whose life and work will remain a source of inspiration to us all.

Faoi mar a dúirt mé tá an dúshlán sin romhainne anois, cinntíu go seasfaidh muid an fód ar son a hanam dílis.

Catherine Connolly
20 November 2005

Catherine Connolly represents the people of Galway as a city councillor. As a councillor and as Mayor of Galway she supported Bríd Cummins in her search for equality and justice. After Bríd's death, Catherine was, at times, the sole public voice seeking answers — for which she was verbally abused and her resignation was demanded. Over the past year since Bríd's death, Catherine has continued to help Bríd's family in their search for the truth. Catherine Connolly is also a barrister.

Bríd Cummins

Bríd was born in Clonmel on 16 February 1956, the youngest of seven children, six girls and one boy. She was educated in Clonmel, and worked in the Civil Service with the Revenue Commissioners in Dublin and Waterford. Having completed a course in journalism in England she worked for *Newsweek* and Reuters, and also lived for a time in Brussels where she was employed in the European Parliament.

Bríd moved to Galway in the late 1980s and spent the last years of her life there — it was a city she loved. She was involved in drama, art and poetry, and helped to produce and act in "Hatch 22", a play about Galway's unemployed. She edited the ground-breaking *Simon Anthology of Poetry* in 1988 which included poetry from Ireland's leading writers in aid of the Simon Community. Bríd completed a four year course in homeopathy. An accident in the mid-nineties affected her health. She subsequently suffered a lot of back, neck and facial pain, and also suffered from depression — all of which curtailed her creative life and ability to work full-time.

After losing her battle with Galway City Council, Bríd was evicted from her flat in Munster Avenue. She was found dead in her flat on 6 December 2004 on the day the bailiffs came to evict her.

Bríd was a very intelligent and talented person with a social conscience. She never reached her full potential.

Bríd's last words to her family were that she felt she had let down the people of Galway who didn't have a voice or the ability to campaign for justice.

May she rest in peace.

The ritual made me cringe
You didn't notice.
You would have loved it
Daddy.
Streams of sad faces came
To say goodbye.
You looked so calm,
Your torment over.
I envied you, and wondered
At the feel of your frozen,
Lifeless skin. Still tanned,
Soft.
But that was no longer you.
A body in a monk's habit.
You were already in my
Heart.
I wondered what the point was.
Does God have to be asked
Over and over, to have
Mercy on your soul?
Didn't you pray all
Your life, for salvation?
Yours and ours?
Especially mine!
It seems I know you
So much better now
Understanding comes too late.
Do you know me now?
Has understanding come to you?
Can you hear me when I
Call for you?

He climbed abroad the train
In his new coat.
He looked smart and neat,
Just like the gangster
He was.
I had to steel myself,
To stop from asking him
To stay. Forewarned
By the gloom of
That train-station goodbye,
I hurried home and
Locked the door with
A deft finality.
Another chapter closed.

No celebrations, but
Many tears. My life
A constant puzzle.
If I ever rewrite
This play, I will have
A walk-on part only.
No more leading roles.
There are just so many times
To get up again.
Only so much smiling
Is painless.

Rise Up Now

*Last Friday night's meeting to 'Save St. Joseph's Hospital'
inspired Bríd Cummins to pen the following poem.*

We gathered in our hundreds
We were full of hope,
We listened to the speakers
Thought of offering some a rope!

We shivered in the cold.
As we stood outside the hall.
We cheered and clapped for some
But surely not for all.

The doctor said his piece
Angry Widows put their case
The Workers Party had their man
He was put in his place!

Politicans came to mind their seats
Could what they said be true?
Or was this just another farce?
Well known to me and you.

Cashel or Clonmel? That's the question
I know whose side I'm on
It will be too late to voice support
When Old St. Joseph's gone.

So rise up now and shout out loud
Say what you feel for all to hear
March, protest and show strength
Or for your silence, you will pay dear.

Lost in that enormous bed where
Once my grandmother died, I
Watched shadows become monsters.
Shapes of the Christmas crib became
A crouching killer on top of the
Wardrobe. Flowers on curtains
Became faces of evil and
Laughed at my terror.
I lay dead centre, so
The rats who crept in with
The dark wouldn't bite my hands
Should they dangle over the edge
In sleepy abandon. I wanted
To turn on the light, to break
The spell darkness brought, but
Every now and then, a downstairs
Door opened, as my father came
Into the hallway to check.
The merest chink would have
Given me away.

If that man next door
Hammers another nail
I'll hammer him.
I'll take him on
A snowless sledge
To oblivion.
Where he can't lay his
Restless hands on
A single tool.
And the rust will
Make his joints creak,
But I won't hear them.
And bit by bit
The house he built
And rebuilt
Will stretch and sigh
On warm summer days
And whisper "thanks be to Gods"
The hammer man is gone.

Now the dancing girl
Can float in the
Limbo-land next door
And no longer
Hit the wall, or
Hit the roof, or
Hit the bottle.
And the hammer and nails
And drills and saws of
The hammerless man
Will go to rust and
Bother us no more.

His bed was in the corner,
By the window.
I held his hand,
Death flickered in his eyes.
He said he was afraid of
The gap in the curtains,
So the nurse pinned them
Together.
He imagined the throb of
The heart monitor
Was the sound of footsteps
In the gloom.
He was afraid
Afraid of death,
Afraid of life,
Afraid of love.
I was afraid
Of him.

One crazy night, you
Teetered on the lip of life,
Your lethal hands gripped
The balcony railing as
You swayed outward. How
You loved to taunt, while
I sat calmly inside
The window below, and
Told you to jump! To, for
God's sake – but mostly mine –
Jump!

Four floors down, the
Stray cat's kittens romped
In the landlady's garden.
I feared you'd squash them.
'Go find your mother, little ones'.
'Don't let the bad man hurt you'.
My cried were drowned by your
Hysterical laughter.
The garden was now clear.

So tired. I rubbed my temples
And thought maybe the moon
Did this to you.
When you changed your mind,
And finally went to bed,
I lay awake.

There are many cats on my roof.
All colours, all sizes,
They stretch in the languid sunshine
And wait to be fed.
I long sometimes to be one of them,
An independent observer.
Their sleepy eyes deceptively imply
Total relaxation,
But their highly-sharpened senses
Stir them into movement
At the slightest intrusion.
Their sudden leaps and streaks
Flash me back to nightmares
Of claws tearing at young arms
On a summer afternoon:
In a garden that no longer exists,
A cat that no longer exists,
Given to me by a man who
No longer exists.

I didn't know what came to me
In love's cloak.
It sat on the stairs and waited;
So anxious to meet me,
So keen to truss me up,
To influence every moment.
It waited around corners
Crouched in doorways, ready
To spring on my unsuspecting
Vulnerability.
It crawled through the long grass
On sticky summer nights, and
Sat by the river on frozen winter
Afternoons, when fools venture out.
It held me close.

On dusty city streets,
There it was again, with
A mysterious look from dark eyes,
Under a dipped hat.
It followed me through parks,
And flattered me, with offers
Of the high life.
For short periods; I succumbed,
But never comfortable
With disguise.

MOTHER

She spreads her love
Her strength
Her compassion
Throughout the family
All her living life
Loving
And guiding us
Smiles
With ready smile
Smiling.
No task too much
No load too heavy
Weighing.

Always there ready
To listen
She listens
Listening.
So understanding
So patient
So giving
Giving.
Deep thoughts
Wish words
Flow from her
Thinking.
Age seeking to alter
Her beautiful face
Beautiful.

Thickly curling
Silver hair

Graces her head
Gracefully,
Making her stature
Statuesque
Tall, grey-haired
Lady

Her warmth
So warming
Comforts
Comfortingly.
Her laugh
Cheers us all
Cheering
Cheerfully.

She's lovely
We love her
Lovingly lovely.
Loving thoughts
To a loving woman
Heart-gladdening.
Inspirational
Certainly she is
Ever inspiring.
Loved mother of mine
Forever loved
Eternally.

PARTY

Flowing waves of sunshine bathed us in their light
As we gathered together to celebrate, it was a lovely sight
Our old blossom-laden apple tree was our parasol that day
We ate and drank, we sang and talked, while the boys were
    at play.

They ran and laughed, kicked the ball, sending it out of sight
Over the hedge, under the car, into the air like a kite
It sailed, as everyone cheered, with great good humour
A special day for a special person, my 70-year-old mother.

She was unaware of the preparations, had been kept in the
    dark
My brother took her for a drive, up the mountains, 'till they
    parked
And Mam remembered a funeral taking place nearby
So off they went to attend, while we at home did sigh
We prayed and hoped that nothing had gone wrong
And tried to keep cool and fresh, the banquet for this hungry
    throng.

At last the car returned, such excitement filled the air
We ran out, were ready to welcome her, our guest of honour
    was there
Oh no! another delay, someone had stopped to talk, to moan
Quick! An excuse to get her in, tell her she's wanted on the
    phone.

Finally, there she stood, the woman we all love so much
Her face glowed, she was thrilled, her shyness made her
    blush
Her astonishment at finding us all waiting just for her

In party mood, with smiling faces, we really caused a stir
Everything went so well, it was such a wonderful day
Blue skies, happiness, love all around,
that special Sunday in May.

I tried not to look
But her icy glare sought me out.
She couldn't find anyone
More hateful than me.
She wanted to stamp on me.
Among the eggs and empty shelves
Of that just about to close
Perpetuity, she wanted
To flatten me and slide me
Through the slot of officialdom.
To be rid of me.
To shut me up,
Staple me,
File me away.
She can never forgive me.
I asked her for a receipt.

A meter ticked ominously
In the tiny hallway,
A reminder of the tick-ticking
Of that monitor in the hospital ward
Where he closed his eyes and
Offered up his spirit.
The world is shot out.
A bundle of discarded newspapers
Lie on the floor, reminders of
Tragedy.
Nature's beauty dies daily
So that these informers of
Death and destruction
Can lie on floors
In sad rooms.

From a bright sunny morning
To a dim, dark night,
I have returned
To await a revelation,
Or a storm-filled hand
Through a rent in the clouds,
To whisk away the mist
From across the bay,
Which has invaded my mind
So that all I hear is
The ticking of the clocks
And meters, and monitors
Of this world without end.

Her rage split the sky
And caused the stars to hide
In terror.
Her voice startled stones
In distant streams.
Instead of beating him,
She beat his car.
Her face bruised
With betrayal,
She howled at the
Father of her children.
Somewhere, across the fields,
A donkey stirred and
Offered her his broad back.
'Come with me', he said.
'I'll not betray you'.
But revenge savaged
Her heart, and she tore
That once-kissed love.
While the donkey wept.
For lost innocence.
And trust.

Poor little lamb
Bleeds all over
My plate
I lap it up
All that blood,
Just as they lap up
My blood
As I bleed all over
This town.
They soak it up
Spew it out.
My blood.
This time I don't
Lap it up.
If I can't swim
Through it,
I'll part it
With one swift command
And
A raised hand.

I remember Brussels,
Wednesdays when the flowers died,
the coffee and croissants mornings,
ritual trips to Sunday markets,
alien accents,
Arabs.
We sat separately on a trundling tram,
trapped in each other.

Those eyes I once loved,
wanted me to smile.
But I couldn't,
though I knew you needed it.
Too much pain wormed its way
around my heart, my mouth,
As I lived in a shapeless world
of no decision.

I remember the smell of mint
oppressive on the air;
the tumbling thousands of brightly coloured
oranges, pineapples, melons,
cobbled spaces overrun
with befrocked swarthy men,
wailing strains of Persian music,
the clacking, bumping of overhead trains.

We packed provisions for two
into the straining check trolley,
picked arguments about nothing,
frustration tensing our faces.
Teeth ground back vicious words

of truth and untruth.
Laughter smashed through barriers of anger,
to release us for a time of closeness.

Weighed down by the exhaustion
of hating and loving simultaneously,
we replaced insecurity with food and goods
we would never need,
our torn, bruised souls
cheered by armfuls of flowers,
bought cheap before closing,
to die at home.

RETURN TO SENDER

Rita Ann Higgins

One woman against the letter of the law
  IRISH TIMES 18 December 2004

(Bríd Cummins was found dead in bed
on the day she was due for eviction, 6 December 2004)

Our acting city manager
never stops acting.
he never stops playacting.
He's a rule-book carrier.
he letter-of-the-laws it.
he jaw-jaws it.
He praises and praises,
his full of humanity staff,
his staff who gush with kindness,
his staff who sing while they work,
his staff who say, good morning,
how may I help you?
Free from blame all the same,
a councillor said, exonerated,
they are all exonerated,
staff exonerated he said it again.
Another councillor said policy
policy, policy, we have to carry out council policy.
Galway city council policy.
We have to letter-of-the-law-it,
we have to jaw-jaw it.

Good staff, lovely staff,
full of humanity staff,

gush when we walk staff,
gush when we talk staff,
Staff exonerated, all exonerated.
Policy policy, letter of the law, all jaw-jaw.

Clever letter-writing member of humanity staff
writes great letter bereft of hope,
sends great letter bereft of hope
to emergency housing authority 'Cope'
telling Cope to spare the hope this Christmas.

Don't re-house her
when we evict her,
the clever letter writer wrote
in a clever letter sent to Cope.
A clever letter bereft of hope.

She answers back.
She calls back.
She's a trouble maker.
She's riddled with anti-social behaviour,
She claims a back injury,
She's always looking for repairs,
and if it's not repairs it's a transfer.
She's taking legal action against us.
She pisses us off
and us dribbling with humanity.
we gush when we walk.
we gush when we talk.
we are exonerated.
A councillor said so,
exonerated, staff exonerated,
we were carrying out council policy,
Galway City Council policy.

Our acting city manager,
our playacting city manager,

playacts on our behalf.
He has a duty to protect his staff.
He has a duty to protect his back.
He knows how kind we are
all year round
but especially at Christmas.

*Rita Ann Higgins read this poem at an evening in
commemoration of the life of Bríd Cummins*